Boy from Burma

Boy from Burma

Carolyn Crain

Pilgrim Spirit
COMMUNICATIONS
Tacoma, Washington

CONTENTS

PREFACE

ONE OF THE MATERIAL THINGS I wanted to inherit from Dad was the four-drawer mahogany file cabinet that he had since his early days in the ministry. By the time I did claim it in 2001, it was full of written materials. He seldom wrote out a sermon, but he kept rough notes of them, and also kept with them the bulletins of the church services he had led. Newsletters from the churches in Oakland and Seattle, copies of family trees going back to the 1600s, occasional newspaper clippings, letters, cards and some of his poetry swell the manila folders in every drawer. It is a vast archive to be sorted, assessed for usefulness in my writing, and either discarded or kept. It is difficult for me to throw away anything from people I have loved and want to remember. Perhaps this is a shared human trait and the file itself is testament to it.

For much of my life I have felt grateful for the people I have known and experiences I've had. Looking back over my eighty years, I am aware that my satisfaction has been due in large part to my father, Richard Cummings.

There are so many reasons why that is true, and since I decided to write about him, I have been remembering and pondering those reasons. I have wanted to know more not only for myself, but also to try and share him with others. I expect that family members who knew him will be interested, and enjoy hearing his story. More than that, I hope the story is rich and well enough told to interest anyone who finds this book in their hands.

So here it is, my attempt to present my father in words and some pictures. I hope that you will enjoy meeting or remembering him, and that he will bring a smile to your lips and warmth to your heart.

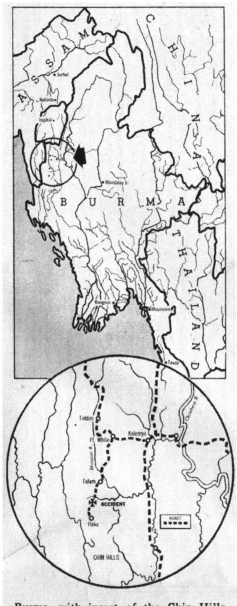

Burma, with insert of the Chin Hills
and area traversed by mission group.

*Magazine cover with Bob Johnson, Ram Hlun, and
Dick Cummings at the hospital in Falam, Burma.*

Near Death in the Chin Hills

THE JEEP SLID OFF THE JUNGLE ROAD and dropped down the hillside about twenty feet before it crashed into a tree and rolled onto its side, having dumped out its passengers. One of those passengers was my father, Richard Cummings, who landed on his back and quickly realized that he could not move his legs. The man who slowly stood up and started walking through the jungle vegetation toward Dad was his colleague, John. Farther up the hill lay missionary Bob Johnson, unconscious and losing blood. It was a bad scene on a rainy night, sixteen miles from the nearest village in the Chin Hills on the western border of Burma.

It had started well enough, this tour of mission fields in a country now called Myanmar. It was early 1954, and Dad was with six other staff people related to the ministry of American Baptist Churches (ABC). John Skoglund and Hazel Shank were "foreign secretaries" from the ABC headquarters in New York where Erville Sowards worked as well, in charge of the Burma mission. Mrs. H.G. Colwell was a past president of the American Baptist Convention. Having spent a week in the Rangoon area with the Kachin people, the group flew in a DC3 to the small village of Kalemyo for a visit with the Chin people. There they were met by missionary Bob Johnson and his family's cook, Ram Hlun. The two women were to visit Tiddim; the men to travel farther to Haka.

The Chin Hills are actually mountains—ten thousand feet

high—on the western edge of Burma bordering Assam. Missions had been established in three separate villages. Dad, John, Erville, Bob, and Ram climbed aboard a converted army truck which, in Dad's words, "jounced out of Kalemyo on a road that rises seven thousand feet in the first twenty miles." They slept that night on cots in a public bungalow at Pine Tree Camp, where the air was clear and the temperature about fifty degrees.

It was chillier the next morning and hot coffee was a welcome comfort. Ram, the cook, also prepared eggs which were polished off before the group squeezed back into the jeep and headed for the village of Falam. Arriving at the Manipur River at about noon they found the small wooden cage, suspended on a steel cable, by which they would be carried across the water, there being no "jeep-able" bridge. Instead, four men on either side of the river operated the winches which pulled small groups of people, limited to five hundred pounds at a time, across the river in the cage. On the other side were two jeeps which had been rafted across in the previous dry season. These vehicles were available for hire along with an Indian driver.

Picture a rough roadway gouged into the side of a four-thousand-foot mountain by laborers using large hoes. This road had to be maintained daily, as landslides occurred almost that often, making it impassable. The frequent switchbacks required the driver to back around twice on some of the corners as the road rose another thousand feet, before arriving at a bridge across the Pau River. The jeep started its climb up the steep grade on wet road recently covered with loose dirt. It was ten o'clock in the morning. In Dad's words:

> "The driver started up and made it to within eight feet of the top. When he tried to shift into a lower gear, the jeep slipped backward. It slid

to the right and dropped vertically for 20 feet. John Skoglund fell out at that point. Sowards, Johnson, and I were carried or rolled some 30 feet further. The jeep had spilled out all of its occupants by the time it crashed into a tree. Bob Johnson and I were on the ground and helpless. Ram Hlun, the cook with us, was badly hurt. Sowards and Skoglund could stand up, but were in pain. Only the driver escaped injury."

The first person to act was Hlun who realized that Johnson was unconscious and losing a lot of blood. Despite his own injuries, he began climbing uphill to the next village. Collapsing three times before reaching Tiphul, he finally found people to come and help. It was raining on the jungle terrain by then, and the injured men were very grateful for the air mattresses and blankets that were brought, and the cots which they were able to retrieve from the jeep. A chicken was cooked on a small stove and soon broth and coffee were ready to help warm everyone.

In addition to the physical help they were getting, the men were grateful that the Christians among the villagers prayed with them as they made plans to get back to the shelter at the Pau River, then to take Bob and Dad on to the hospital in Falam. Litters were fashioned from bamboo and vines, and with eight men carrying each one, they made their way back down the road. It was five in the afternoon and growing dark, so torches made from pitch pine were lighted, burning intensely enough to withstand the rain and send a pungent resin smell into the damp air.

The litter bearers hoisted the patients off the ground and "grunting in unison, they climbed for 35 minutes." They were met by a second relay of men who would carry them on. Eight miles from Falam a crowd of fifty people was waiting, members

of the Christian Endeavor Society and the Boy Scouts who had
hot soup and two gasoline pres-
sure lanterns. It was now two-
fifteen in the morning. When
they finally reached the little
hospital, the injured men could
at last shed their wet clothes,
wrap in warm blankets, and re-
ceive treatment with penicillin,
morphine, and shots for typhoid
and tetanus. It would be seven-
teen days before they were able
to journey back to Kalemyo, and
thence to Rangoon. Bob would

In body cast Dick Cummings continues
schedule. "Headdress" is a palm tree in
Carl Capen's yard, Bangkok, Thailand.

have to travel back to the U.S. for jaw surgery, and Dad would
be swathed in plaster casts—one covering most of his torso for
a broken vertebra, and one on a broken ankle. Indomitable
spirit that he was, he decided to travel to his planned stops in
Bangkok and Japan before heading home.

Among my memories of that crisis is being called out of
class at Nyack High School and told that Dad had been in an
accident, but was going to be okay. At the time I was not much
aware of Mom's feelings although we knew she was worried.
I think she wanted to shield us girls from the fears she had.
I doubt that she was very pleased about Dad's decision to
continue the trip, but she must have kept that to herself, too.
When he finally did arrive back in the U.S.A. she had an am-
bulance meet him at the airport in New York City to bring him
home. I had never seen anyone in a body cast before, and it
was both interesting and kind of scary. Mostly, we were all
immensely happy to be together again.

One of the treasures from the trip, which now belongs to me, is a pine torch, signed by the men who used it to light the path in the jungle on that terrible night. Dad's summary of the experience:

> "The heroism of Ram Hlun, the sturdiness of the stretcher bearers, the quick sympathy, the generous giving, the concern and devotion of the Chin people, our brothers in Christ, thrilled us with a vision of spiritual living that is possible even in the here and now. We were very near to the only kind of life worth living."

My paternal grandparents, Dora and John Cummings

Boy from Burma

RICHARD CUMMINGS HAD neither a middle name nor a birth certificate, and although he celebrated his birthday on the seventh of October, he used to say that he might have been born on the eighth. The family joked that his parents might have run out of middle names by the time this sixth child was born, in 1910, in the village of Henzada, in southern Burma, halfway around the world.

My grandparents, John and Dora Cummings, were missionaries appointed to the country of Burma by the American Baptist Board of Missions. During their many years there they were responsible for the building and operation of schools as well as directly preaching the Christian gospel. Grandpa was known for making tennis courts wherever he was living, and Grandma's letters spoke of the vegetables that she was growing, such as celery. Together they produced nine children who, as they became old enough for school, were sent back to the United States. They lived in a home for missionaries' kids in Newton Center, Massachusetts. The woman caring for them was Mother West who, according to all of Dad's stories, was a wise, warm and wonderful person. In his words:

> For the wisdom and loving care of Mother West I shall be ever indebted, for she was mother to me in every sense of the word. Every evening after supper, the whole family of children gathered in the living room for prayers. The simple services

were usually planned by the high school children. We all took a lusty part in the singing and sooner or later, joined in the scripture and prayer. Religion at the home was joyous as well as serious. And we learned that it had to do with washing dishes, mowing lawns and controlling bad tempers as well as going to church on Sunday.

Mother West

When Dad's father John set out for Burma, he was following in the footsteps of Dora's father, William Roberts, who had sailed for Burma in 1878 to minister to the Kachin tribal people in the northern part of the country. He established a church and built a house in the village of Bhamo, and at one point along the way, sent for his daughter Dora, by then a graduate of Vassar, to come and keep house for him. She agreed and embarked on what was then a long journey. On the boat she met the young man named John Cummings who was returning to Burma for a second seven-year term of service. His first wife had died from typhoid there, and he had taken their three young children back to live in Massachusetts. I don't know if the six-week journey was enough time for John and Dora to fall in love, but by the time they arrived in Rangoon, they were definitely interested in each other. So, instead of keeping the Roberts home, she married and established her own home with her husband John in the southern part of the country.

The most famous story about Great-grandfather Roberts concerns his seeking permission from King Thebaw, who was ruling Burma at the time. I think that he expected to meet with Thebaw, but was ordered to crawl across a courtyard on his hands and knees, and then stop and kneel with his hands over his eyes. When his curiosity got the best of him, as later reported, he spread his fingers enough to see three mingyees, or court officials, sitting in a row. In his own words, Great-grandfather reported:

> One of those august ministers was shaving himself with a pair of tweezers—for they pull out rather than cut off their beards; another was preparing a chew of the favorite betel nut and coon, pasting the soft lime-mortar on the leaf with his fingernail; the third, with his mouth so full of this coon that he could not speak, was using a square hole in the floor as a spittoon.

The missionary's request to be granted some land was translated and considered at length. Finally they informed him that there was no land available inside the stockade, but he could request land without, and they would petition and recommend that King Thebaw grant it. Knowing that the Kachins were a dangerous tribe, he nonetheless headed back to Bhamo

Family reunion at Newton Center, Massachusetts

August 1945 - Reunion of brothers Bill (far right) and Dick (left of Grandfather Cummings) and their families.

to choose a parcel of land for the mission compound. Eventually church and school buildings were erected. I stayed there in 1959 when I visited Burma, and other relatives have been there since. I recently received some pictures of a busy school yard full of children. It would warm Great-grandpa's heart.

Returning to our story about Dad in Rangoon, Richard was being called "Dick." He was a happy child with curly brown hair and blue eyes, who learned Burmese words along with English ones. In a letter back to some of the older siblings in the United States, his mother said:

> I wish you could see little Richard at this age. He is full of life and talks Burmese far more than most native children of his age. William Henry talked earlier than the rest but Richard has beaten him all hollow. He says anything in any language that is spoken to him and is stuffed with Burmese, Karen, English and Hindustani in turn.
>
> He doesn't look as if he suffered from mental strain either. Since our cow calved and we are getting good milk again he has grown so fat that it seems another ounce added to his cheeks would make the skin burst. He has a beautiful mop of fair curls, which I suppose his father will hate to have cut . . .

Dick had older brothers Roger and Bill, and older sisters Ruth, Dora and Carrie. Rounding out the family were younger twin girls Clara and Lora. With so many children and no English-language school available there, the family was separated a lot of the time. Missionaries in those days were furloughed only every seven years, so once the children were in the U.S., they had only letters from their parents and those could take two or three months to arrive. The family story is that they were all together only once, for Thanksgiving Day in Newton Center.

When I was about eight years old, we drove from New Hampshire over to the cottage that Grandpa then owned in York Beach, Maine. We pulled into the grassy drive and saw another car there. Dad took a look at the license plate and yelled "Maryland! It's Bill!" It had been years since they had seen each other, and obviously, they had seldom been in touch.

Grandpa's cottage, near York, Maine

Dad was brought back by his parents when he was about four years old. He was given into the care of Mother West and attended schools in Newton Center. The sibling with whom he had the most time during his elementary school years was Bill, who was two years older. We loved hearing stories about their times together, mostly the ones about summers in Maine. One of the three children from Grandpa's first marriage was Bess. She and her husband Bud Walden owned a farm in Greenville and the children spent days with them quite often. A favorite pastime there was to slide down a roof that sloped low to the ground. Once when a neighbor chided Uncle Bud, saying how bad that was for the roof, he replied, "Yes, but it's awful good for the kids."

If adults' attitudes influence kids, Dad may have caught his uncle's. Certainly he developed the habit of saying something positive at the end of a sentence, even if the thrust of the conversation was about troubles and problems. One of the friends he had in the later years of his life called him "pathologically optimistic." However, his happy attitude was a big influence on me, and I am grateful to have his aptitude for seeing the good side of things in this life.

My mother, Barbara Hamlin Cummings

My father, Richard Cummings

Mom and Dad's wedding on August 17, 1932 in Milo, Maine

THE LOVE OF DAD'S LIFE

DAD GRADUATED from Newton High School in the spring of 1928. Having been accepted at Colby College in Waterville, Maine, one of his father's alma maters, he entered that school in September.

The story goes that Dad, as a student at Colby in 1930, was walking on campus one spring day when he noticed a young woman hitting golf balls beside a dorm building. He was intrigued by her energy (and presumably her looks), so he asked around to learn her name. "Barbara Hamlin," he was told, "and she is really smart." That did not dim Dad's interest. The next time he saw her he smiled and struck up a conversation that would last for fifty-four years.

The woman who attracted Dad was about five feet six inches tall, slender and light complected. The platinum blond hair she was born with had gradually become light brown, and she wore it cut short. Because her blue eyes were very nearsighted, she had worn glasses from the age of six.

Mom was a born student, getting straight A's with a minimum of effort. Following her graduation from Milo High School in the middle of Maine, she went to Boston to attend Lasell Seminary, a junior college for young ladies. When she graduated as valedictorian in 1928, the line beneath her yearbook picture read, "Her academic record reduces us to despair."

From the time she was able to read, she was checking out piles of books from the Milo library, first children's stories, and later historical fiction and poetry. She wrote poems and stories, some of which were published in school magazines. An introvert by nature, she was more likely to spend time by herself than with groups of people. She had only a few close friends who really knew her well. She joined the Chi Omega sorority at Colby College, but sometimes took pleasure in sitting in a prominent spot on the porch while her sorority sisters went off to meetings.

Her academic success continued at Colby where she earned her Phi Beta Kappa key and wrote a valedictorian speech for the third time in her life, having also been valedictorian at her high school as well as Lasell. She graduated a year ahead of Dad in 1932.

Dad's first car

Dad's first car was a Model T for which he paid all of twelve dollars and fifty cents. He must have been thrilled to have his own vehicle, and I know that he didn't waste any time getting on the road north in Maine to visit his sweetheart. His trip along the two-lane road went smoothly until he was within a few miles of his destination, when the car broke down and he had to phone Barbara, whom he called "Bobby" in those days. His future in-laws—who were well-to-do, living in one of the nicest homes in town—had to go rescue him and (presumably) pay for the necessary repairs. Not an auspicious entrance for a suitor!

On one of his subsequent visits to Milo, Dick took the formal step of asking Carrie and Ed for their younger daughter's hand in marriage, and received their blessing. During the summer, plans were made, a wedding party of ten arranged, and the big day arrived. The wedding at the Baptist church in Milo went as planned with Dad's parents among the celebrants. The bride and groom attended the reception, but ran off before friends could pull any pranks on them. They loved the outdoors and headed not to a fancy honeymoon suite, but to Moosehead Lake where they loaded up a canoe and paddled out for a week of island camping.

It was Dad's plan to become a full-time pastor, so the newlyweds headed to Andover Newton Theological School near Boston. Their new life was a drastic change for Mom. Her father—who had been orphaned at a young age and pretty much raised and educated himself—had done well financially. The house that he had built to occupy with his wife and five children was one of the finest in town. Mom, as the baby of the family, did not lack for nice things, such as handmade silk dresses and fine furniture. It was said that Grampie once stepped into the hallway from her bedroom saying, "There are twenty-eight pairs of shoes in this closet!"

I know from letters and other evidence of Mom's life before marriage that she was very active and energetic. She loved the snow of Maine winters and pursued skiing, ice skating and using her Norwegian "kicksled." One of her favorite stories was about her taking her mother for a ride on the new sled, a present for her twelfth birthday. The kicksled was basically a one-person seat supported by metal struts between long, thin runners, with a handle on the seat back. The operator stood on the runners behind the seat and kicked off with one foot to get started. Mom got her mother, who at that time weighed over two hundred pounds, to walk to the top of the highest spot on the road into town, covered with hard-packed snow. Settling Grammie on the seat, Mom stood on the runners and said, "Here we go." She had no idea how fast they would gain speed, and she quickly got scared. Halfway down the hill, she said they were flying and she had no control. She was terrified, but said nothing to her mother—whose hat had flown off— as they sailed to the bottom of the hill and slowed to a stop. Breathless at first, Grammie finally looked up and said "Well, Barbie, you handled your sled very well." I'm pretty sure that was the last sled ride they took together.

Mom with her kicksled

Mom's journal describes being outside after school almost every day during her high school years, involved in winter sports until it was dark. Those evenings often ended with Mom making a big pan of her favorite chocolate fudge with walnuts. In the summer she often went on hikes. She climbed Mt. Katahdin which is about a mile high, the northern end of the Appalachian Trail. She was a strong swimmer, often swimming in one of the nearby lakes. She learned to paddle her brothers' and father's canoes, drove the family car, and loved it all.

One of Mom's rare fishing trips

As a young married couple headed for the pastoral ministry, Mom and Dad had very little money, and no expectation of a lavish lifestyle. Mom was so in love and glad to be with her sweetheart that she was ready to live differently and, after seminary, moved happily into the little apartment upstairs in a Cambridge house, the first home for me. By the time my sister Barbara was born five years later, the church had purchased a house across the street as a parsonage for us. I think Mom was happy to have more space and a fenced yard for her children.

I do not recall Mom participating much in play, such as the winter sports she had loved in Maine. I think that she had a stereotypical picture of a proper 1940s pastor's wife which was refined and reserved, and she acted accordingly. Her New England upbringing and family lifestyle probably made that easier for her than it would have been for many other women. She did not even drive the car, as the man usually did that, so Dad was always behind the wheel of our black Pontiac. It is sad to think that she gave up so much, and it was sad for us girls that she did not join in many playful activities with us. Over the years in the pastorate, Mom became depressed. She had no really close friends, and was isolated in the parsonage.

Mom continued to be a student, reading a lot and beginning to write outlines for Bible studies in the field of Old Testament prophets. Her favorite was Amos, and drawing on her seminary education, she turned the studies into adult Sunday School classes that fascinated her students. Finding that she enjoyed the role of teacher, she soon gained a reputation for her skill, and other churches began asking her to speak to them. One such church was a Negro congregation (yes, we still used the word then). That pleased her because she had learned an attitude of racial fairness from her own mother, who was ahead of her time in rural Maine.

I remember Mom reporting that the offering was taken after she spoke. The ushers brought the plates to the front and set them on the big table. The pastor proceeded to count the money, then announced that it was not enough, and asked that the plates be passed again. The second time the total was enough to satisfy him and he put all the money into a big envelope. Turning to Mom, he thanked her again and gave her the entire offering. To say that she was mortified barely described the moment.

*My maternal grandparents, Edwin M. and
Carrie B. Hamlin on their 50th anniversary.*

One of Mom's favorite holidays was Easter, and she looked
forward to the celebration each year. She combined her writing skills and love of poetry, and planned an Easter basket
hunt for me and Barb. Outside our bedroom doors we would
find baskets containing only a piece of paper with a poem di-
recting us, through hints, to other locations. When we found
the next location, there would be another note, so we went
up and down stairs, looking into cupboards, under furniture,
behind doors, and once, I remember, in the dryer! Usually
we had to follow six or seven notes to the longed-for baskets
filled with candies, gum and other goodies. Often there were

tall chocolate bunnies at the center. I loved those baskets, and kept the little poems from one year to the next.

Another thing that I loved was the reading that Mom did with us on a regular basis. Both Dad and Mom read us bedtime stories, but when we were sick—which could mean just a cold—we were confined to bed all day, and Mom would spend a lot of time reading us stories. Sometimes it was the same one over and over, such as my favorite about the Thanksgiving Squirrel which was in book number II of the Home University Bookshelf. I still have the red bound volumes of that set in my bookcase. Other favorites of all of us were the Thornton Burgess animal stories which brought foxes and bears and deer to life. At the top of the list was Winnie-the-Pooh.

Over the years Mom had a variety of physical problems: phlebitis in her leg, bursitis in her shoulder, and worst of all the subarachnoid hemorrhage which was a major turning point in our family life. That type of bleeding which occurs in the space between the brain and its covering, causes a sudden severe headache. She was treated with strong pain medication, and it was not until I was married and had our first child that she began to overcome the addiction which she had developed to pain medication. Life was difficult for Dad and for Barb during her high school years, when I had already left for college. However, in words spoken at Mom's memorial service, this is what Dad had to say:

> It seems that in this life the gifts of great mental capacity, of extreme sensitivity and of high spirit are a fragile combination against the rough-and-tumble of this world. And now and then the rough-and-tumble were too much for Barbara. However, in our fifty-three years together, I would never have given up the brilliance, the

loving empathy, the high free spirit in exchange for simple good health.

In the ways that count the most Barbara was God's ministering angel in my life, bringing richness and meaning and blessed truth. We were fortunate that we could talk together about our faith in the love and purposes of God. I want to tell you about one such wondrous time. We were in Maine, driving to Brownville Junction at sunset. The whole sky was ablaze with flaming red clouds. It was so beautiful we stopped the car and watched in silence as the color faded, and the purple shadows came. We spoke together the words of a poem that Barbara had loved and taught to me:

After Sunset

I have an understanding with the hills
At evening when the slanted radiance fills
Their hollows, and the great winds let them be,
And they are quiet and look down at me.
Oh then I see the patience in their eyes
Out of the centuries that made them wise.
They lend me hoarded memory and I learn
Their thoughts of granite and their whims of fern,
And why a dream of forests must endure and how
Though every tree be slain:
Invisible beauty has a word so brief
A flower can say it or a shaken leaf,
But few may ever snare it in a song
Though for the quest a life is not too long.
When the blue hills grow tender, when they pull
The twilight close with gesture beautiful.
And shadows are their garments and the air
Deepens, and the wild veery is at prayer,
Their arms are strong around me, and I know

That somehow I shall follow when you go
to the still land beyond the evening star,
Where everlasting hills and valleys are
And silence may not hurt us any more,
And terror shall be past, and grief and war.

~ Grace Hazard Conkling

Mom and Dad on their 50th anniversary

DAD'S NATURE

NOT LONG AFTER DAD DIED, I contacted a psychic who was recommended to me by a friend whose son had died. I was hoping for some sense of Dad in his afterlife, whatever that might be. I had previously had a very positive experience with a different psychic following the death of a man I loved, and I had found some peace in that.

Perhaps I should have listened to my misgivings when this new person suggested that we meet at a Borders bookstore. The branch I had worked at did not have much private space, but I trusted that the person knew better than I, as she had met with clients at the location close to her. She was waiting for me on the second floor where there were some comfy chairs, but I still felt a bit exposed.

She already knew that I wanted to talk about my father, and started off by saying, "Your father was a rather stern person." I immediately wanted to say "NO, you have contacted the wrong man. HIS father was stern, but not my Dad." Instead I said, "No, he wasn't stern." She went on to suggest that she was just sensing that he could be serious, and we continued to talk. The most positive thing that came out of the session was her answer to my question about whether or not his experience after death was what he had expected. Dad and I had had many long conversations about life and death, and he had come to the conclusion that there was probably not a life after this one on earth. Her answer was that his experience was different than what he had thought. Although I was not feeling very confident in the psychic, I did think that there must be some sort of ongoing spiritual consciousness, and Dad must be living in that.

Recalling my time with the psychic, I puzzled again about why she felt that he was a stern man. I don't think that I had mentioned his being a pastor, but maybe I had. I find that people have a preconceived bias that ministers are about hellfire and brimstone, ready to hit you over the head with the Bible. The crossword puzzle I did today asked for a word meaning a pastor's subject. The answer that fit was "sin." It is surprising even to me that given both my parents' conservative backgrounds, they had become open-minded, progressive-thinking people for whom faith was a positive and adventurous life.

My father was a positive, happy, energetic, non-judgmental person. His blue eyes sparkled in his long face, and his feet sometimes danced as well. He loved singing and telling stories, and had a loud in-breath kind of laugh. He was generous and full of compassion, and these qualities made him a well-loved pastor. He liked reading, and especially loved poetry. He and Mom sometimes read out loud to each other, and he wrote some poems himself. He was intelligent and curious. Whenever he traveled somewhere on a plane, he came home telling stories about the people sitting next to him, what they did for work, and all about how the job was done and who was in their family.

Person-to-person learning was easier for him than formal education, so he was not the Phi Beta Kappa student that Mom was, and his spelling was atrocious. I still have a small cardboard box from his tool collection marked "bitts." He tended to procrastinate, and told me that he once had to write 100 times "Procrastination is the thief of time." for one of his teachers. He said it took him a while to arrange three pencils in his hand so that he could write three sentences at once!

For Dad's memorial service, Barb and I created a photo display which we titled "A Wonderful Life." In one picture he was diving into the swimming pool that he had in California; in another he was on skis in Maine—so many examples of the energy and love of life that characterized him. In writing about Dad, I want to portray him accurately, bringing to life on the page the wonderful life that he lived and created for me and my sister.

Dad with his granddaughter Alissa.
"Alissa is going places!"

Alissa, in highchair, telling Dad,
"It's a funny secret!"

Pretty serious discussion with grandson Nick

Celebrating graduation with granddaughter Pam

THE JOY OF WOOD

O N THE WALL above my spinet piano hangs an intricately carved piece of natural teak wood, about four feet wide and fourteen inches high. There are four distinct horizontal sections divided by thin strips of wood. The main section, about six inches high, is carved completely through the piece, leaving open areas around big leaves. The three smaller sections are carved only deep enough to create stylized flower buds and smaller leaves. I had never seen this heirloom until Dad gifted me with it after I bought my first house as a single person in 1990. "This came from a bazaar in Rangoon," Dad said, "where it hung on the street front over the row of stalls. My father brought home about twelve feet of it. I have been keeping this piece ever since he gave it to me in Newton Center. It really was quite a project to dust all of this design, and as you can see, I made two end pieces to finish it off for you."

I was much pleased with this gift, the beauty of the piece, and the work Dad had put into sprucing it up. Soon it hung over the stairway to my favorite second-story room from which I could see the rich design against a white wall. As I did, I pictured Dad with a small stiff paint brush removing years of dust from the light brown unfinished teak wood. It must have been tedious, and yet I think he enjoyed doing it. Dad loved wood, admiring the beauty of its grain, the fascination of the knots it formed, the smell of it as he walked through a pine forest, or later, as his saw cut into it.

I wonder when my dad first became interested in wood, appreciating both its living and cut forms. Perhaps it was a natural outgrowth of his learning to identify trees, a skill which he would pass on to us girls. In his early years in Burma he must have seen teak growing, and sometimes watched as elephants moved it about from the forests to the carts that carried it to markets or work sites. Maybe he wondered what it would feel like to perch atop the big beasts as the mahouts did, shouting directions.

When we would drive in the car up north into New Hampshire for summer vacation, Dad would point out all the different trees that grew, the great variety of shape and size. The conical pines and firs provided a beautiful dark background for the deciduous trees, especially when the New England fall painted the brightest foliage in the country.

It didn't take that degree of splendor, however, to interest Dad. He taught Barb and me to identify the blue spruce and the stately elms that were plentiful before the Dutch Elm beetle came. I think he and I liked the white birches best, with their pristine white bark and the amazing ability to bend their trunks nearly to the ground. Both he and Mom could recite Robert Frost's poem about them.

When I was about nine years old Mom began to collect some antiques and we would sometimes drive to auctions. Mom's interest was primarily in pressed glass, but Dad would look at the furniture, admiring the beauty of the grain in something like quarter-sawn oak. I would look at the wood with him, and I learned to distinguish between the grains. Walnut was dark; pine light with more knots. Some maple was dotted with "birds' eyes," and some called curly. I remember being very pleased when I correctly identified the wood in a desk as cherry.

I loved sitting in this big wooden swing chair with Mom.

My earliest memories of Dad and wood include the smell of hot linseed oil being heated on the big wood stove in the Deerfield house, and then being rubbed with a soft cloth into the round top of an oak dining room table. I think Mom and Dad had found the table at an auction. We hauled it home in the open trailer which we pulled behind the car when heading to and from the Deerfield place for our six weeks of vacation each summer. Dad refinished the table and delighted in moving it to the dining room where we ate all our meals together.

The other thing that delighted me and my little sister was when Dad would plane a piece of wood, creating thin strips which would curl as they left the tool. We would pick up the curls and try to make them stay in our hair in different styles without breaking them. If it had been a contest, I would have won easily as my curly hair hung onto every piece, whereas Barb's slick, straight hair would quickly send them to the floor. Dad would laugh with us and admire our efforts at coiffure.

He also showed us how to use the plane, and emphasized the need to keep our fingers well away from the set-in blade.

In later years, after the Deerfield place was sold, Dad began to draw out some designs for tables, and collect pieces of wood with which to make them. These pieces, some as big as five feet in length, were stashed under beds or in garages, moving with my folks as they migrated from the East Coast to the West. One of the pieces of apple wood became an end table supported by legs of Washington madrone wood. A big piece of walnut was transformed into a coffee table to grace my sister's living room in Michigan. When Dad and his wife Agnes moved into the retirement community in Santa Barbara, there was a wood shop on the campus, and Dad seemed excited about the amenities there, but in fact he seldom used them. He preferred to work alone, I think, at his own pace in his own space. I now have a small table which he made; it has thin crooked legs with the bark still on them. It stands beside a couch in my TV room reminding me of Dad's whimsical side.

Dad with my sister Barbara and me
at the Deerfield, New Hampshire house.

It was to that side of him that I gave an unusual gift one Christmas—not very practical, I think, but fun. In a wood shop in Oregon I found a neck tie made of many different slices of wood, polished to a shine, and hung on a leather thong which hooked at the back of the neck. Each piece that hung below the knot was a little wider than the one above, so that the tie was the proper shape, narrowing again to a point at the end. There were slices of dark walnut, light birch, yellow oak, white pine, Oregon myrtle, and some I had never heard of before. Upon opening this gem, Dad's face curled into an amused grin, wide-eyed and open mouthed. "Oh, my gosh!" he said, "This will be fun."

All dressed for church

Sharing the Faith

I AM A READER, particularly enjoying contemporary writing about the world's religions, progressive Christian faith, and spiritual life. As I get excited about the latest book I find myself wishing that I could talk with Dad about the ideas or questions that it raises. He loved talking about such things, sharing his own questions and how they shaped his faith. Many evenings when we were visiting together, we would sit up until eleven or midnight enjoying the chance to share openly and without judgment.

As a parish minister he preached, of course, on most Sunday mornings. I knew that he spent time each week preparing what he would say. Mom told me once that early in his career she would help with the writing of sermons, but came to a point when she wanted let him do his own preparation. Even so, they continued to share with each other about Christian life and how to live it.

I looked at him in the pulpit, proud that he was my father, and glad when he smiled. He did that a lot—his face was very expressive as he spoke. My brother-in-law said that Dad was a very engaging speaker, right from the first word out of his mouth. He was buoyant and joyful, with a dramatic flair, and he had respect for his listeners. In a conversational style, he drew from simple everyday things that had gotten him thinking.

I remember one sermon well, probably because it included an incident that had happened at a concert we attended the night before. The artist was a well-known German woman pianist who played with great passion, eliciting much applause. As we were walking out a woman behind us said to her companion, "Wasn't that a marvelous concert? She played with such power and feeling."

"Yes," was the reply, "but did you see the horrible green dress she was wearing?"

I had actually been fascinated by the dress. It must have been satin, as it was shiny and elegantly long when she stood after each piece. I had thought it beautiful.

What Dad took away from that snippet of conversation was that it matters how we use the word "but" in a sentence. "What would you remember," he asked, "if you heard, 'I thought her dress was horrible, but she played so powerfully and well.'" I was surprised that he made a sermon out of putting the positive thought on the right side of "but." And I still remember it, eighty years or so later.

Another time I remember him starting a sermon by asking how many people remembered a hymn which said, "Will there be any stars, any stars in my crown?" Then he moved from stars to scars, asking, "What hurts have you suffered that left either visible scars or invisible ones?" Most scars don't require treatment or any kind of attention, actually. Hurts are inevitable, of course. Some of us are inclined to pick at our hurts, keeping the healing process at bay. Allowing them to heal and leave scars is the better way. As gross as it seems to me now, when I was small I used to pick at small scabs, and was scolded by Mom, who told me it would make a worse scar. That didn't stop me, however. Scars tell parts of our stories and display our ability to endure. Many of us develop pride in our scars.

Dad often used such mundane things as he developed his sermons. He rejoiced when he connected with his listeners, and they resonated with what he wanted to convey. On the other side of the coin, he listened well, and people sought him out to hear their worries and ponderings. There was no judgment on his part, none of the "fire and brimstone" often attributed to preachers. There was respect and genuine interest and a gift for linking common experiences to the good news of the gospel.

Interestingly, he was less likely to extend that grace to himself. He would sometimes express frustration with his lack of discipline and his procrastination. Looking at myself, I think that I inherited those challenges, but I also know that I learned kindness, acceptance, and patience as a listener—skills which I put to work in my career as a counselor.

Dad enjoying a boat outing with nephew David

Dad in his early years, ready for the slopes

Winter Adventures

THERE WAS A SMALL BODY of water called Beldon's Pond not far from our big parsonage home in Troy, New York. Being shallow, the pond froze quickly early in the winter, and we had only to walk across the street and a couple of blocks down the hill to get there. At the edge of the pond there was a small building warmed by a little wood stove, providing a place to rent skates or to take a break and warm up. What with the stove and the sawdust on the floor, the place had a woodsy smell. It was comfortable and also featured a counter where you could buy penny candy and cups of steaming hot chocolate. My favorite candies were the little foil cups like mini pie tins, maybe three inches wide, full of a white, sweet taffy-like concoction. With each one you got a small wooden scooping stick.

Dad wore his baggy wool pants and a red and black plaid jacket. Sporting black skates with long blades on his feet, he'd slowly venture out onto the ice holding my hand on one side and Barb's on the other. He encouraged us to straighten our ankles and push off on one foot. After lots of falls we began to manage a few strokes and to laugh together, proud and happy to be with our father. When our feet got too cold, we would go back to the hut and rest a few minutes before walking back home. Then he'd help us take off the smelly wet wool, putting mittens and socks on radiators and rubbing our feet with his hands, warming our souls as he did so. I loved those days on rented ice skates with my sister and my Daddy.

Later, when I was ten years old, I was given a pair of black skis with white trim. They had only a toe strap to hold them onto my black rubber snow boots, so I had to work hard to climb up the hill without slipping out of them. Bamboo poles with wide circles of webbing at the bottom helped me do the herringbone steps, back up the slope. It was tricky to keep the points of the skies out to the sides, at about a forty-five degree angle.

It was a rare treat for me to be with Dad for a day without my little sister, and I treasured those times. I was so grateful for his patience, even as he skied down to retrieve an escaping ski and climbed back up to help me strap it on. His breath puffing clouds in the cold air, he would smile and say "Let's go again, honey." With snow sticking to our wool pants we'd whoosh back down the hill. It would be considered a bunny hill, but to me it was high adventure and I never wanted to go home, even when my feet were numb and my woolen mittens soaked.

It was nearly forty years later when my sister and her husband Rick invited me and Dad on a trip to Whistler in British Columbia, Canada. Dad was in his seventies, and had slowed some in energy and stamina, but not in enthusiasm. Barb and Rick had rented a condo for a few days between Christmas and New Year's. Accompanied by their children Pam and Nathan, who were older teens, they came to my Tacoma home. Dad joined us from California and we headed north in two cars.

A world class ski resort, Whistler/Blackcomb offers downhill runs and also cross-country trails. Rick and Barb, being experienced skiers, had brought equipment for both the Alpine runs and the Nordic trails. They had intended to purchase some downhill lessons for me, but I felt too scared to accept their offer. Instead, Dad and I decided to go cross-country skiing at the bottom of the mountain, he using Nathan's skis. I had brought my own. Unfortunately we learned that there was not enough snow on the lower half of the mountain that year, so we were directed to the gondola for a trip up to some other Nordic trails. Swinging in the little glass cage off the cables made me a bit nervous, but we arrived safely at the top where big flakes of soft snow were falling.

Trails there were, but they were very slick with hard ice and I quickly realized that I would not be able to ski. I worried about Dad. Surveying the scene, and not to be deterred, Dad said "I'm going to head over here off-trail and see if the going is easier." He stepped off beside the trail, waved and smiled and moved his right ski ahead. I watched him swing the poles until he disappeared from sight over a slope perhaps a hundred yards away. I wondered how steep it was on the other side, but didn't venture after him. The temperature was about twenty-five degrees, so I shuffled around trying to keep warm as I waited. I thought about other cold adventures with him and realized that we were in the process of switching parent/child roles. I felt responsible for his well-being, and resentful that my sister was off on the downhill slopes and not there to help keep an eye on him.

After about half an hour I began to worry, scanning the area where Dad had gone. I removed my skis and sat down to wait and watch. Finally I saw the blue knit hat appear, then the tan parka. Lifting each leg very slowly, he emerged over the edge of the slope and waved at me. I walked toward him until we could hear each other. His words, coming in gasps, alarmed me. "Honey," he said, "I think I am in trouble." Because he had had a heart attack a few years prior, I was afraid that he might be having another. His breaths were labored and he spoke haltingly between them. I said "Let's sit right here." Once he was off his skis and seated, I set out to get help.

The ski patrol hut was on the other side of three lifts dispatching skiers, so—slipping in my cross-country boots with their stiff soles—I had to dodge people coming off in all directions. Finally reaching the patrol hut, I was greatly relieved to see a young man there who must have seen my anxiety. "My dad needs help," I said. He immediately jumped up and said, "Come on, we'll get the snowmobile." It was my first ride on one, but I didn't enjoy it much as my heart was pounding with exertion and fear about my father. When we reached Dad, the patrol guy helped him onto the machine and headed for the hut. I trailed behind on foot, and got there as Dad was stretching out under warm blankets. They strapped on an oxygen mask for a few minutes, listened to his heart and let him rest until he regained normal breathing.

When we agreed that he seemed okay, the ski patrol guy walked to the gondola with us and rode down the hill. "You know," he said, "the altitude here is over seven thousand feet. Next time you should come up and sit in the lodge for a while before you ski." Dad's eyes started to twinkle as he smiled and said quietly and with some humor, "I don't think I'll be doing this again." I didn't hesitate a second before saying "Not with me, you won't!"

MANY TALENTS

DAD WAS A MAN of many talents and he was always ready to learn a new skill when it was needed.

In about 1943, Grammie and Grampie helped Mom and Dad purchase a huge old house in Deerfield, New Hampshire. Built in 1776 as an inn on the stagecoach run between Portsmouth and Concord, it had neither running water nor electricity. Dad studied some books and consulted with some people more experienced than he so that he could plumb and wire the house. I wanted to help him whenever possible, and he was patient showing me how to use the basic tools: hammer, saw, screwdriver, and pliers.

He once gave me the task of watching the ceiling in the dining room at Deerfield as he drilled for wiring on the floor above. He wanted me to yell when I saw the drill point starting to come through from the third floor. I don't know whether I looked away for a moment, or he was turning the hand drill really fast, but by the time I saw it, there was a sizable hole. I yelled and he came down to look. "Well, honey," he said "at least we know where it is!" Eventually the hole was patched and the wiring completed.

The inn had once had a bar with a serving window opening to the side yard. The one-time bar became a bathroom complete with a shiny new tub. I remember being intrigued with the faucets. They were round and solid chrome, one with a blue circle and one with red to distinguish cold from hot. I definitely remember how nice it was to sit atop a porcelain toilet rather than perch over a hole in a wooden plank in the drafty outhouse. I had been haunted by stories of a woman who was butted in the behind by a goat which had somehow wandered and become stuck under that corner of the shed!

Despite the faux pas of an enthusiastic young child, we completed many projects, so we enjoyed indoor plumbing as well as electric lights. Remembering those projects made me think about all the different hats Dad wore during his lifetime: husband, father and pastor; violin player, swimmer, fly fisherman and camper; farmer and flower gardener, conscientious objector, music lover, golfer, philosopher and a storyteller. And in all the frustrations which arose in these various activities, I seldom saw him angry. He would say, "doggone it" or "Jehoshaphat." I heard him say "damn" only once, when a loaded wheelbarrow overturned on the hillside in Nyack, New York sending all the just-raked leaves tumbling.

Carla, a friend from the retirement center where Dad lived in California, once dubbed him a "pathological optimist." To me as a child he was just a happy man, smiling and laughing and making the best of everything. Negative comments were usually followed by "however" leading to positives. From holes in the ceiling to tomato worms in the garden to camping in the rain, he always found the sunnier side. I remember him making pancakes for my sister Barbara and me on a camping trip, undeterred by the rain falling right into the fry pan over the camp fire.

He was my hero.

The Deerfield house

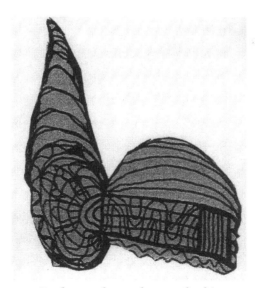

Dad was always known for his doodles—just another of his many talents. This is his take on a Burmese man's hat, called a "gaung baung."

The old Ryder place that Mom and Dad owned in Brownville, Maine

Cold Christmas

I N December of 1960, our whole family decided to travel to Maine and have an old-fashioned Christmas at the vacation place my parents owned. I was pregnant with our first child, fitting for a young woman at that time of year. Dad and Mom, my sister Barbara, my husband Warren, and I drove north from Rochester, New York up through Vermont. The trip was smooth until we got to the town of Dover, Maine, oh-so-close to our destination of Brownville. It was dark and snowing hard by then, and the roads were so icy that we couldn't make it up the hill. With my mother saying, "This is terrible for Carolyn," and me responding, "Mom, I'm fine," Dad backed the car slowly down the slight hill, and tried again to get enough traction, but the tires spun in vain. The people from the nearest house came out to see if they could help, and invited us inside to stay warm. After a cup of hot coffee, Dad and the family's father went back outside to spread some ashes around the wheels. After a few more tries, Dad felt confident that we could make it, so we climbed back in and finally conquered the hill. Dad said, "Isn't it ridiculous that we could get all the way to Dover and then get stuck?"

The old Ryder place, named for a doctor who once lived there, had neither central heat nor running water. When we first walked in, it felt colder than the outside air which was about twenty degrees. There was a big wood stove in the kitchen and fireplaces in each of the other rooms. Warren and Dad began making trips to the woodshed; they soon had several fires crackling upstairs and down.

The privy was in a shed beyond the woodshed, so we had to brave the cold again before heading to chilly beds. The only things that eased the pain of frigid linens were the bricks that Dad had warmed on the kitchen stove and wrapped in towels to put at our feet. The temperature continued to fall during the night, and hovered around zero the next morning.

Mom's agenda was that we go out and cut a tall balsam fir tree to decorate. "It must touch the ceiling, you know," she said, with a smile in her blue eyes. Not anxious to brave the cold, we lingered over a breakfast of bacon and eggs, toast and coffee. Finally Dad stood up and stretched in his red flannel shirt, donned his coat and hat and headed out to the shed. When he returned with a mischievous smile on his face, he was carrying the toilet seat. "RICHARD, what are you doing?" Mom asked loudly, and then couldn't help laughing. "Hanging this up behind the stove," said Dad, "so you can carry it out with you nice and warm. You can't do your business sitting on a block of ice!" What a riot!

Back to the business of the tree. Dad decided that we would use the old moose sled—a wooden affair with solid upright boards forming runners which curved up toward the front—to haul the tree out of the woods. Warren stuck his head out the door to check the thermometer and reported, "Hmm, it's moderating. It's up to five degrees above." With the sun shining on a glistening world, we began putting on layers of clothes, boots, scarves, and gloves and headed out to find a twelve-foot tree. Beyond the door yard, as it was called, was a large raspberry patch and then open field. On the north side of the house was a stand of pine but we headed back farther into the lot to find the proper kind of tree for a Maine Christmas to please Mom.

We considered several before we agreed on the right tree, tall and full, and the men proceeded to saw into the trunk. It smelled so good, fresh evergreen wood in the cold air as the fir was hoisted onto the sled and secured with some white rope. We were all glad to tromp back through the snow and get out of the penetrating cold. Mom had remained in the warm kitchen, and offered a fresh round of hot coffee. Then it was time to stand the tree in the front living room and trim it. There were a lot of ornaments familiar to me from childhood, but perhaps the best thing was a tiny red sock Mom had chosen for our baby who would be born in May. It hung beside bigger wool socks from the mantle above the fireplace, a promise of new life amidst a loving family.

Mom filling stockings at Christmas 1959

Dad working in his composting bin

In the pumpkin patch with his youthful helpers

BUNDLES OF STUFF

G IVEN HIS ENTHUSIASM for gardening it is no surprise that Dad loved compost. Even before he acquired a chipper/ shredder to use, he was chopping up various vegetable matter: kitchen scraps, grass clippings, fallen leaves, and in Santa Barbara, seaweed. He recycled some graying boards into a composting bin up on the hillside across from his unit at the retirement center and in the California heat, he soon had rich soil to shovel from the bottom of the bin.

Always on the lookout for more fodder, he prevailed upon the grounds crew at Valle Verde to leave grass clippings for him on the blue tarp he spread out on the proper day. Then he would draw the four corners together, hoist the bundle from the ground, and sling it up over his shoulder. As he moved through his eighties his stride shortened and his steps slowed, but he made it up the shrub-covered hillside on the indistinct path to the garden plot and dumped the precious cargo into the bin.

As time went on Dad's friends began to help in the composting efforts. One woman who was a member of his church asked if he would like to add some manure to the mix. She was a petite Chinese woman in her seventies who dressed stylishly and drove a white Cadillac. It quite surprised Dad the first time she called to say she was stopping by. He was watching as she drove up to the curb, got out, opened the trunk, and lifted two bags of steer manure from her impeccably clean car before he could even get out there to help. It pleased and amused him.

Once when my friend Lucille went with me to visit Dad and Agnes, we said that we were going over to walk on the beach a short distance away. Dad's blue eyes lit up and he said, "Oh, maybe you would bring some seaweed back with you." Rising from his gold-colored recliner, he went and got two black plastic yard waste bags from the kitchen closet. Smiling, he said, "Seaweed is wonderful fertilizer, you know." I did know, and I also knew that there were some forty-two wooden steps down from the cliff drive to the beach. That was the easy part, of course. It was the forty-two steps back up hauling heavy wet seaweed that were the challenge. We did it of course, filling the bags with as much as we could lift, climbing slowly and appreciating the three little landings built out from the long stairway. Were the designers rock hounds, or were they composters?

The results of all this labor were so worth the trouble people took. Dad raised tomatoes, corn, beans, carrots, squash, and lettuce. One year the local school district contacted the retirement center to ask if some children could come and learn about gardening, and Dad decided to participate in the project. He decided that pumpkins would be a good thing to grow, and three fifth graders were assigned to work with him. The young boy and two girls came several times and helped him get the soil ready. That included working in some compost, of course, and then planting seeds. They weeded and watered and watched the blossoms form on the hairy vines, then laughed and shouted when the first small fruits began to appear. By the time Halloween was approaching, it was decided that there would be a contest to see who had grown the biggest pumpkin. Dad needed the children's help to get the biggest of theirs into the rusty blue wheelbarrow and trundle it downhill to the weighing table. Everyone there was impressed by the size of the thing, and then truly blown away when it registered a whopping forty-six pounds on the scale. Dad's team had won!

My father not only grew prize pumpkins and other edibles, he had flowers everywhere. My niece once remarked that if you were looking for Grampie's house you just needed to look for the most flowers. He had white chrysanthemums, red geraniums, yellow zinnias, and of course a variety of roses. These all benefited from the compost Dad created and spread around. It is not surprising then, that the last things he loaded onto the moving truck when relocating for the last time were two large black plastic bags of wonderful compost.

Dad with his prize-winning pumpkin
—all 46 pounds of it!

A "PR" photo of Dad

OUT OF CHARACTER

I WATCHED A MOVIE last night which was about a dog and his attachment to his human through several dog lifetimes. The movie brought back a disturbing memory. My sister and I, probably in our twenties then, were riding with Dad on a country road in Maine. We were going to spend a day at the beach place owned by some of my mom's relatives. We had stopped to buy some donuts and were enjoying them in the car when suddenly a cat ran across the road in front of us, followed by a small black and white dog. The cat made it, but the dog didn't, in spite of Dad's braking when he saw the cat. We hit the dog, who flew off to the side of the road into the weeds where we couldn't see it anymore.

We all yelled, "Oh no, Oh my God." I expected Dad to stop, but he continued on. "Dad," I said, "we should stop and tell the people in the house we just passed." I was shocked when he said, "No, I don't want to stop and get mixed up in that." WHAT? This is my Dad who goes out of his way to be kind and thoughtful, fair and just? I didn't know what to say, and apparently Barb didn't either, as she was silent. In fact the silence remained until we had gone a few miles and approached the next town. When we resumed talking, it was about the common things we were passing, houses and flowers, country stores, and children playing ball.

It was a long time before that sad event faded out of my thinking. I had never seen behavior by Dad that seemed so callous, and I didn't know how to fit it into my image of the father I loved so much. The few times I thought about it I could understand not wanting to get "mixed up" in people's grief and reactions to losing a beloved pet. I wouldn't have liked stopping, delaying our time at the beach, maybe helping them look for the little dog, and of course nothing would bring it back. But it was the act of moving on, avoiding the situation, and not facing the facts that seemed so out of character to me.

I have tried to think of other such experiences, but have not remembered anything quite the same.

My usual experience was of Dad going out of his way to extend understanding and concern to folks. After all, that is what the pastoral ministry is all about, isn't it? I also remembered an incident he had related to me some years before, about when as a young boy he threw a rock at a squirrel on a telephone wire. To his surprise it hit the little animal, which fell to the ground and remained motionless. Dad was filled with remorse, and it was the last time he threw rocks at anything alive.

The difference, of course, was that he chose to take aim with a potentially lethal weapon and death resulted. Plus you can't go and find a squirrel's family to apologize.

I wanted to make excuses for Dad acting out of character. The world I grew up in lent itself to seeing life in black and white. I was protected from "bad" things, risk taking, and the darker side of life. I remember once on a train trip to Maine when I was about seven years old. We had a compartment, our own little room for sleeping overnight. When we were getting ready to go to bed, two men were standing in the aisle outside our door. They were arguing and getting louder and louder. When they started swearing, Mom opened the door and told them that she had young children who shouldn't be hearing bad language. The men walked away and we had our pleasant environment again.

At various times when were together over the years, Dad and I spent a lot of time talking about such things as difficult choices, and philosophizing about the way life is. Along the way, I have learned, as all of us do, that much of life is lived in shades of gray. Maybe it was that knowledge that came into play that day on the road in Maine.

A Most Happy Fella!

MUSIC

WHEN MY SISTER and I were clearing out Dad's home after he died, some of the hardest things for me to leave behind were the two hundred or so vinyl LPs of music in the hall bookcase. Many of them were Broadway shows, full of songs that he enjoyed—and which he would occasionally sing and get people to join in with him. I have vivid memories of the day he took me and my best friend Eleanor to New York City to see the movie *Hans Christian Anderson*, and how he loved that music. He was especially delighted by the two-part "Inchworm," and we would later sing that together, weaving the two themes as best we could. I carry a feeling of warmth with me still thinking about that show.

In Detroit, he and my sister Barb and I went to see *The Most Happy Fella* and came away imitating the Sicilian accents of Tony singing "In Palermo, Mama, when I was a young boy . . . " I can hear Dad's baritone voice now, coming through his smiles. He so enjoyed clever lyrics and joyous tunes.

I felt a little sad, sometimes, that my mom did not share that love of music. She once said that music was powerless to express emotions adequately. She preferred words, especially the poetry that she read and sometimes penned herself. I appreciated—and probably inherited from her—the love of words, but I couldn't understand how she could not like songs and marches and the haunting beauty of instruments like cellos and oboes.

On typical Sunday afternoons, following the work of Sunday School and worship at church, Dad would lie on the couch after dinner and listen to Beethoven's Fifth Symphony, soaking in the richness of the orchestral sound, and only occasionally falling asleep. He often hummed as he worked on projects in his many gardens. Almost always the songs were happy ones, but he also loved several Negro spirituals like "Go Down Moses," and seemed to feel the yearning for relief and freedom that they expressed.

When Dad was in high school he learned to play the violin and was in the school orchestra. He carried the instrument with him and started out in the orchestra at Colby College, but someone stole his violin, and he was unable to replace it. When he told me that, I felt sad and angry at how wrong it was to take that away from him. Perhaps that is why, when he was in his seventies and expressed an interest in my playing the guitar, I bought a second-hand guitar and sent it to him. He was thoroughly surprised, and intent on learning to play. He soon found, though, that his fingers didn't work well on the strings, and he would hit two at a time. Eventually he gave up on that effort, but he never stopped singing to his heart's content.

I remember being occasionally embarrassed by his impatience with people who played too slowly, especially if they were accompanying hymns at church. He thought music ought not to drag, whether on the piano or the organ. He would mutter under his breath, "Come on, come on, speed it up." Or he would just raise his voice a bit and sing faster, coming in a beat ahead of the accompanying instrument, to say nothing of the congregation which was almost always behind the beat. I was not sure at times whether to sing with him or with the organ. I was glad that he did not do that from the pulpit with a mike.

One of the places where we most often sang was in the car. When we lived in Troy, New York, we owned a summer place in Deerfield, New Hampshire, a drive of about four or five hours at that time. Mom did not join in the songs, but she did tolerate our singing everything from show tunes to the old popular songs like "Daisy, Daisy" or "I Want a Girl (Just Like The Girl That Married Dear Old Dad)." When I reached high school age and was listening to the countdown of popular songs, we would try some of those. When we got tired of singing, Barb and I would play the "animal game," counting cows, horses and occasional goats, each on our own side of the car. It was Dad who made the extra fifty points available to anyone who saw a grind stone in a field or barnyard.

Once on my birthday, Dad surprised me with the gift of a 45 rpm record player and the recording of one of my favorite songs, "Moulin Rouge." I really appreciated that present and the validation it was to me of the value of music. Dad's appreciation of music is a gift that has blessed me all my life, and I have been enriched by listening and singing—by myself, in high school and college and church choirs, with my children, grandchildren, and now with the great-grands. What a gift!

Mom's well-worn cedar recipe box,
with one of our favorite recipes

The Pleasure of Food

ONE OF DAD'S GREATEST JOYS in life was the eating and sharing of good food. Of course there is always debate about which dish is the best, and how to prepare it. Husbands and wives do not necessarily agree about cuisine. In our house, the dinners centered around some type of meat—Mom's favorite being roast lamb—served with vegetables like corn, green beans, carrots, and sometimes beets. The starch was almost always potato, usually baked, as that was Mom's favorite. We never lacked for desserts, often made from Hamlin family recipes. Mom had a small cedar box, a wedding gift from her sister Edna, which held three-by-five inch cards. On each card Edna had written a family recipe, creating a wealth of cooking history passed down through the years.

Mom's love of chocolate meant lots of brownies, "Spry chocolate cake" with fudge frosting, "kiss pudding," which was a custard with chocolate meringues floating on top, and of course, chocolate chip cookies. She made the best pie crust using lard—which really does outdo any other shortening— and we didn't know the dangers of cholesterol back then. Dad enjoyed all of these treats and often asked for a second "small" helping. He was especially happy when the pie contained apples off our own trees.

My father would have been more adventuresome, I think, had he been doing the cooking. He enjoyed rice, and would have been glad to eat it more often. He also liked fish and was pleased when Mom made a chowder using salt cod, which she had to soak in fresh water before cooking with it. I loved it too, mainly because the cod came packed in a little wooden box with a cover that slid off one end. I can still smell the salty fishiness that stayed in the box for a long time. Of course Dad liked to eat the fresh trout that he caught when we were in Maine. Those he would usually cook himself in Grammie's black cast iron frying pan on the big wood stove, and serve them for breakfast. Mom never did enjoy eating fish due to its having bones, so she stuck with such favorites as bacon and eggs and home fried donuts.

Dad was such a people person that he would always invite others to join us for special meals such as holidays and birthdays. He seemed to be especially pleased when it was what we would now call a diverse group. I remember a Japanese couple who came for Thanksgiving. He made people feel comfortable, and he truly listened to their stories.

A family dinner at my sister Barbara's house

He was in his element when entertaining at the big Deerfield house in the summer when the corn was ripe. He started by soaking the full ears of corn in a bucket of water for about an hour. Then he got out the little grill, filled the V-shaped metal fire box with charcoal and lit it on fire. When the coals were hot, he would lay the cobs of corn, still in their husks, on the metal grid. Soon steam would rise from the corn, and the husks would start to curl and turn brown. It smelled wonderful.

"Oh, that does taste so good," he would say, when finally eating from his cob of Golden Cross Bantam, butter and juice dribbling down his chin. Dad was not one to eat quietly. He enjoyed all his food with exclamations and frequent praise for the cook.

Mom certainly enjoyed good food too, but I think that when it came to feeding guests she felt stressed. She wanted to do it properly, which meant having the house clean, and serving delicious food presented on good china with white table cloths and napkins. She tolerated company but was happier when eating with just her family. No matter who was there, however, if something was spilled on the linen cloth she would get a pan from the kitchen and some hot water. The pan went under the spot on the cloth, and the water was poured through the cloth to remove or at least minimize the stain. I found that process quite fascinating.

On one occasion Mom and Dad invited their friends Paul and Tillie over for a New England feast. They had ordered a whole lobster dinner including clams from Maine, and it arrived on the right day, packed in a big kettle. We could tell by the sound that there was water in there too. Having boiled lobsters before, Dad turned on the stove and set the kettle on a hot burner. The table was set, the butter melted, and the guests invited to their chairs.

Dad lifted the cover off the kettle and was enveloped in a cloud of steam that smelled of the Maine coast. His laugh was heard before his head appeared in the kitchen doorway saying "Well, the lobsters are red and the clams are open. We have seaweed, and would anyone like to try a cooked bib or napkin?" Instructions? What instructions?

In Santa Barbara, after Dad retired, he enjoyed going out to two Chinese restaurants nearby. One of his favorite dishes was lemon chicken. In American restaurants he liked to try new things, especially if he was in a different area of the country such as the South, where he enjoyed jambalaya. On the road between New York and Maine there was a Scandinavian restaurant where he discovered a fruit soup which delighted his taste buds.

All along the journey I learned that eating is fun, can be an adventure, and is best when shared with some people you don't know, and the people you already love.

TRANSITION

To say that life is full of changes would be a huge understatement. Some say that the only constant in life IS change. In our family of four there were changes that moved us from one house to another, and one city to the next. They involved changing schools and churches, and for Dad, changing jobs. For him there were also the changes in Mom's health and well-being, some of which took up a lot of his time and energy. He seemed to be determined to make life as good as possible for all of us.

In spite of the hard times of Mom's depression and physical health, I believe that the most difficult thing for Dad was when she had to go into a nursing facility in 1986. He had to deal with the pain of being unable to care for her himself any longer, and also the reality of being alone. He had never in his life lived by himself. I was able to visit him in Santa Barbara for a few days and go with him on the daily visits to see Mom in the nursing home. I will always be glad for that because she lived there for only two weeks, passing away peacefully at the end of June.

Over the years my folks had met many people across the country through the American Baptist Convention (ABC). Dad traveled quite a bit especially as director of public relations for the foreign missions department. Together he and Mom had attended some of the national meetings, often making new friends.

When Dad agreed to serve as interim pastor of the church in Oakland, California, he and Mom moved to a part of the country new to them. They had not been there long before they recognized an old friend in the congregation. Agnes Sherman had lived in Pennsylvania where her first husband had been a pastor. Back then she had worked on the staff at ABC headquarters in Valley Forge when Dad was there. Agnes was a tall, slender woman with the light complexion and hair typical of her Swedish heritage. Her blue eyes showed her friendly disposition and interest in people. Dad described her as a "take-charge woman." She had outlived a second husband and had an apartment near the lake in Oakland. Dad later said the he could not imagine a woman with whom he had more in common. So it seemed natural that one day they would become attracted to one another.

The three enjoyed sharing meals together, went to movies, and while Mom was well enough, even all the way to the place in Maine. Agnes was able to help care for Mom and also to meet some of her family.

After Mom died in the summer of 1986, Agnes was one of the many who were a support to Dad. Over the next few months they spent more and more time together and in the fall Dad shared with me and Barb his desire to marry Agnes. It was obvious in his general demeanor of joy and lightheartedness that he was happy to have her in his life. Not wanting to dishonor Mom by marrying too quickly, they agreed to have the wedding at the end of the year. They were married in the Oakland church in December, celebrating with a number of family members there. Agnes moved from her Oakland apartment to the house Dad owned in Pleasant Hill, where they lived until making the decision to move to Valle Verde, the retirement center in Santa Barbara.

Dad with his daughters, Barbara and Carolyn

Perhaps the most stressful experience there was the wild fire that tore through the area soon after they moved in. It was a fast-moving brush fire that spread quickly, coming within a few feet of the Valle Verde campus, closing Highway 101 and dividing the city. The scariest thing was that they were both away from home at the time. Dad had gone to the grocery store, while Agnes had driven downtown. She was one of many people forced off the road and into a motel for the night by the police. It was about four hours before they knew where each other was, when Dad got home and Agnes was able to call him.

During their ten-year marriage, they made the most of retirement living. They made a trip to China together, and joined a church in Goleta, just north of them. That was where Agnes' daughter and family lived, and get-togethers with them and with the families of Agnes' four sisters living in the area were frequent. They would picnic at the nearby lake, walk the cliff above the beach, entertain friends at home, and together they canned lima beans and plums from the garden. I was so glad for Dad to have that happy length of time when life was more "normal" and fun again. In fact when Agnes died in 1997, I said this at the memorial service: "The thing for which I am most grateful to Agnes is that she chose to spend the last ten years of her life with my Dad."

Agnes and Dad

CATCH OF THE DAY

M Y FATHER WAS A GREAT STORYTELLER and in his ninety-one years of living, he accumulated a lot of material. He delighted in the telling, and friends and family delighted in the hearing. One of the favorites from the Cummings family annals was about his father, John Cummings, and the retrieving of a log for firewood.

Because my grandparents lived out of the country for many years, I don't have a lot of memories of them. I recall Grandma being a rather quiet woman, proud of her long white hair. She was probably about five feet six inches tall, not much shorter than Grandpa was. He was of slight built and seemed quite serious to me.

When they retired from mission work and came home from Burma to live in the United States, Grandpa was determined to buy a lighthouse on the coast of Maine, the state of his birth. Grandma, on the other hand, having followed him halfway around the world and there borne him nine children, put her foot down. She was not going to live in a secluded lighthouse on the stern and rockbound coast. I guess it was a compromise, then, when they bought a small cottage facing out onto a picturesque bay at Cape Neddick near York Beach, Maine, with a fine view of the famous Nubble Light. Grandpa wanted it to be a place where his extended family could gather and enjoy the ocean he so loved. A bonus would be the work that assorted people—sons-in-law in particular—might do while enjoying the hospitality.

One such occasion happened while my aunt Clara and her husband Dave were there for a few days one September. It was getting cool, and lighting the fireplace in the evening was almost a necessity. One afternoon, as they sat looking east across the water toward Boon Island, Grandpa spotted a large log floating in the choppy bay. Excited by this potential windfall he grinned and stood up.

"Dave," he said, "we can get that wood in if you will come and help me." As far as I know Dave's thoughts were not recorded, but I do know that he was not a swimmer. No one would fare well very long in the Atlantic water in September. But being the dutiful son-in-law, he set off with Grandpa to launch the little wooden dory which was propelled only by elbow grease applied to its oars.

Grandpa in proper attire
for splitting precious firewood

Dave was a big man, probably six feet tall and large boned. He must have looked enormous in the little boat next to Grandpa's small frame. As Grandma and Clara watched from the porch of the cottage, the boat made its way a few hundred yards out into the bay among the lobster pot buoys and small swells. When they reached the log a struggle ensued during which, at Grandpa's direction, they managed to haul the log— nearly the size of a telephone pole—up and across the gunwales between them. The wives watched with growing concern as the men began their slow row homeward. Soon Grandma said, "Clara, does it look to you as if that boat is settling lower and lower in the water?"

The view from the cottage at York Beach

Shading her eyes with her hand, Clara replied, "Oh, my! Well, yes, it does." And indeed, as the story goes, the gunwales were close to even with the water. It looked as if the log would float off, leaving boat and occupants to an uncertain but likely wet fate.

As luck or the nature of Maine waters in those parts would have it, a lobster man was also watching the spectacle, and turned the bow of his boat toward the dory. It would be fun to know what he might have been thinking, but his actions were enough for Grandma. She turned to open the cottage door. "Come, Clara," she said. "We must heat some water. They are going to need a lot of hot water."

WATER

SOME OF MY FONDEST MEMORIES of Dad are related to some kind of water. He loved fly fishing and was at home standing in the middle of a stream in Maine, even if the water was cold enough to turn his legs lobster red.

Fly fishing could be serious business, but some of Dad's water fun was more active. He loved to go body surfing in the waves of the Atlantic as it rolled into the bay at York Beach. With arms lifted above his head, he'd wade out into the cold brine to about waist height and carefully watch the surface as the waves formed. When he saw a high enough swell he'd turn and start swimming as fast as he could to catch the wave and ride it all the way up onto the sand. He encouraged Barbara and me to try it as well. We would miss a lot, jump up and down, and then start watching for another good possibility. There was a lot of smiling and laughter, coughing on salt water, and sand-scraped knees. What a wonderful lot of fun.

Dad loved swimming in lakes and ponds too. At his last home in California, he had his own in-ground pool in the back yard. It wasn't big enough for much of a lap swim, but he loved to play. He would stand on his hands with just his feet sticking out, then come up with a big smile on his face. He might go under and grab your ankle, then come up and stand so that you could climb up onto his shoulders and then jump off. He enjoyed the first jump in, and was very disappointed when, after his heart attack at age seventy-five, his doctor told him not to do that anymore because of the quick temperature change.

In my earliest memories, Dad's bathing suit was a one-piece affair in a maroon color. I think it was made of wool. I have some pictures of him in that suit with Mom standing on his shoulders, but she didn't do much swimming after her children were born. Dad was the water hero.

He liked being near the water as well as in it, and enjoyed canoeing or rowing a small boat. We usually visited my grandparents at least once each summer in Milo, Maine. There in the middle of the state were many lakes, rivers and ponds calling to Dad to fish them. I was thrilled when I was invited to go with him, anticipating a good time on the water. It was also a time we would be allowed to wear jeans. We called them dungarees back then, but nice young ladies did not wear pants of any kind.

The first step in a fishing expedition was to borrow a canoe, usually Uncle Oscar's green LL Bean two-seater and paddles. He also had the orange life jackets we were required to wear, and a good supply of fly "dope." Dad had his own wicker creel, an assortment of lures, flies and eggs, and a three-jointed brown rod with a cork handle.

Dad with Uncle Oscar and that well-used canoe

When we were going to fish from a boat we also dug worms for bait. That meant going a few blocks away to Uncle Lloyd's greenhouse where there were piles of compost rich soil to dig in. I loved that job, although my grandmother did not think much of me doing it. She'd say "I don't know how you can stand to touch those dirty, slimy things, so UGLY." I liked the fat pinkish brown angle worms and the way they twisted and turned. I did not like putting them on a hook, so Dad did that, saying that he didn't think the worms had much feeling.

Dad was always ready for a fishing expedition.
"This is some good water," he would say.

I remember one expedition on the Sebec River. The river was close by; it flowed right through the town of Milo, was crossed by a bridge on the main road, and was held back by a small dam. I enjoyed just looking at the river, hearing the sound of water running over rocks and splashing over the dam. I was about ten years old then, and very excited that we could actually be out on the water.

Dad was hoping that we would catch some bass and eat it for dinner. He baited a hook and handed me the fairly short black pole. It wasn't long before I had a bite, but I didn't know what to do as the line pulled taut and the pole dipped toward the water. I held on tight, and the fish swam under the canoe, pulling hard so the pole rested on the side of the canoe. The line got snagged somehow, and the boat began to lean. I started yelling, "We're going to tip over!"

"NO," said Dad as he stood up and stepped close to grab the line. "You get the net there and we'll get this one!" When the fish stopped pulling, Dad began hauling the line up, and the fish eventually came to the surface. I was thrilled, but Dad said "Aw, shucks," realizing that it was not a bass, but a pickerel—a small, green, skinny fish with too many bones to be worth trying to eat. I thought it was pretty great that I had caught a fish!

Although Dad enjoyed being on the rivers and lakes in that part of Maine, his favorite thing was fly fishing, typically done in the streams. These smaller waterways meandered through all kinds of terrain— wooded areas of pine and white birch, swamplands, and fields where blueberries grew. Whether Dad's creel was full or empty. his spirit was always full because he so loved the quiet and richness of nature around him.

A happy fisherman at the Boundary Waters

My sister Barbara and I were always among Dad's favorite photography subjects.

PHOTOGRAPHY

I WONDER WHAT KIND of camera Dad used when he first started taking pictures. Did he borrow one from his brother Bill
or from Mother West who ran the home for missionaries' kids
where they lived in Newton Center, Massachusetts? Perhaps
he started off with a black Baby Brownie as many children
did, or an Ansco "Panda" which was my first camera. What
sparked his interest in taking pictures?

I know that when he was at Colby College, he took a lot
of the photos of various groups for the weekly *Echo* newspaper, and also for the *Oracle* yearbook. I remember him saying that on the trip he took to Europe with Mom before I was
born, he used a camera that produced glass lantern slides. I
have a large box of them now, picturing pre-war Germany and
France. They saw a lot of castles and scenes along the Rhine
River, cathedrals and markets. Exploring new places was
something they both enjoyed, and they were always glad they
made that trip before they had children.

He took many photos of me and Barb when we were babies
and toddlers, and on through the years. Mom did not like to
have her picture taken, and seldom smiled when she did, so he
didn't coax many good shots of her. His other favorite subject
was nature, and there are many beauties among the collection I have. At first, they were black and white, of course: a
campsite with a beached canoe, a string of trout laid out on
the ground under some white birch trees and a couple of his

brothers-in-law in their wool pants and plaid jackets; a small group of the Hamlin family—including Mom—on top of Mt. Katahdin's 5,000 foot summit on a summer day.

Once color film was available, he began taking pictures not only for prints, but also for slides. Before his eightieth birthday party, he put together a slide show of his favorite pictures, of both family and nature. The shot that jumps into my mind first shows a single drop of water on a pine needle, back lit by a sunbeam. He also wrote a script for that show, tying some of his faith and philosophy of life into his appreciation of human love and of natural beauty. He considered the natural world, and especially its infinite beauty, to be manifestations of the Holy Spirit, and often metaphors for God's love.

On a trip to Japan during his years working for the American Baptist Foreign Mission Society, he purchased a German Rolleicord camera, then considered one of the finest made. He did not have time to use it before the trip ended, but opened the box when he was back home, as we were all looking at his treasures. That was when he discovered that the only instruction manual was written entirely in German! Mom, Barb, and I all started laughing, as he made attempts to read the words. He had once proclaimed that German was easy to pronounce. "You just have to open your mouth and swallow a tonsil," he said. It did sound sort of like that as he exaggerated the guttural sounds. Soon he had to stop because he was laughing so hard himself, in his hearty out-breath and then in-breath guffaw. None of us ever understood the instructions but he succeeded in taking a great many gorgeous pictures with that camera.

On the wall in my library room is a bluish-gray photo of Mt. Rainier, its snow- and glacier-covered peak framed by several white-barked trees. It was such a clear picture that

Dad could enlarge it to its 14" x 20" size. He had a couple of dozen smaller shots that were enlarged and matted without frames. He would rotate those on the wall in his family room, presenting different scenes over the course of the year. Someday I will use some of those photos, varying them from time to time on the walls in my room, and continue to appreciate his photography skills.

*Dad took this photo of me and Barbara in the wind
at the top of Mt. Katahdin in Maine.*

Dad being helpful on the movie set in Chaingmai.

MAKING A MOVIE IN THAILAND

ONE OF THE LAST MAJOR PROJECTS in which Dad was involved during his career may also have been one of the most thrilling for him. As head of the public relations division of the American Baptist International Missions Board, he was liaison and support person to missionaries on the various fields around the world. One of these mission fields was in Northern Thailand, where, in 1972, a movie was to be made. Called *Feet Upon the Mountains*, it would show work among hill people in and around Chaing Mai, where advances were being made in agriculture, education, and health.

Dad did not star in the movie, but he did spend two weeks in Chaing Mai. Much of the time he rode in a jeep holding a large red umbrella over the camera crew. The still photo of him doing that is one of my all-time favorite pictures of him. Wearing a light-colored shirt and a wide smile, he obviously loved his job, though I'm sure his arms must have gotten tired.

One of the missionaries there wrote in a letter to Dad on the occasion of his retirement,

> I particularly cherish my involvement with Dick in making for American Baptist Churches, the movie *Feet Upon the Mountains*. In Thailand the going was often rough, the days long, and schedules for filming complicated. But in the midst of it all Dick exhibited enormous energy, unflagging zeal, and a cheerful spirit. . . . His loving

heart has reached out in so many wonderful and splendid ways.

Dad traveled to many of the mission fields in his years with International Ministries, but this was the only time that Mom traveled with him. She had a number of physical troubles over the years, but there would be enough time in one place, and enough ease of schedule for her to go to Thailand. One of the benefits of that is that she kept a journal describing their experiences, which Dad had never done. He was always taking pictures instead. Mom's writing relates a lot of shopping experiences, revealing another side of Dad, who also enjoyed shopping, especially for gifts. He appreciated the variety of texture and color in textiles, nicely-turned wood, and pottery. Handmade items such as mahogany bowls inlaid with mother-of-pearl, woven raw silk clothing, and intricately carved ivory scenes delighted him. Many of these items eventually came to us family members, as well as the friends and host families they met along the way.

Mom recorded one amusing experience in Hong Kong:

> There is no heat in this hotel and there was a grid up near the ceiling that was pouring out cold air. Dick called the desk and was told that they would fix it. Then Dick decided he could fix it himself. He climbed on a chair and from there to the bureau and shut off the cold air. A few minutes later an old woman came with a long stick having a nail on the end of it. Dick tried to tell her it was fixed but she didn't understand and she opened it again! Dick shook his head at her and as soon as she left he closed it again. In a few more minutes a man appeared with a big step ladder and the old woman. Dick tried to tell him it was fixed but the man climbed up and

took off the whole grid. He gave a sharp order to the old woman who went and got an armload of newspapers. He stuffed the hole with newspapers, put the cover back on, said "no more cold," and then disappeared.

The room warmed up, and my parents had a good laugh. I am happy that Mom included this in her journal; I know that both of them were grateful for the trip together, sharing the excitement of the mission work in the hills of Thailand. It was a successful endeavor all the way around.

Mom and Dad sharing a happy day

Dad was always happiest in his garden.

Apple-Pear Jam

IN EVERY PLACE where my parents lived Dad had some kind of garden. In the city settings like Troy, New York or the suburban setting that was King of Prussia, Pennsylvania, the growing places were small. He carved out a section of lawn to create a flower bed and planted spring bulbs in various colors and shapes of pots. Sometimes in early spring he would cut small branches of shrubs like forsythia to force into early bloom in the house. I loved the bright yellow color on the table by the window when the outside branches were still looking brown and dead and the glass panes were cold.

It was in Deerfield, New Hampshire, where we had an acre of land surrounding the house, that he cultivated a large vegetable garden. In addition to all the vegetables we grew, there were fruit trees which came with the property. These included some old varieties of apple trees producing Gravensteins, Transparents, Pippins and some McIntosh. Each ripened at a different time, so there were always apples ready to pick— from the "earlies" ripening by July through the Macs ready about when we were packing up to go back to New York.

I enjoyed apples, usually eating them skin and all. It was also fun, though, to watch our elderly neighbor wield his pocket knife and see if he could circle the apple, removing the skin in a spiral without breaking it. We did rinse the fruit, since Dad had sprayed the trees to prevent worms. I can see him now in his khaki-colored work pants and blue cotton long-sleeved shirt, a small galvanized can strapped to his back and the protruding hose in his hand. He wouldn't let us be outside when he was spraying, and he had a big white handkerchief tied around his nose and mouth. We would all be appalled now to think of using that pesticide—Rotenone, as I remember. But he was determined to have the land produce everything possible. I was too young then to know that he was worried because he was a conscientious objector to the Second World War. If the church did not approve of that stance, he feared he might be out of a job. The more food we could produce, the more self-sufficient we might be.

It was a boon to Dad's gardening efforts that the man who ran the Troy Built Rototiller Company was a member of the church. He invited Dad to go see and try the machine for himself. Daddy was amazed by the power of the contraption and the speed with which it could turn over the soil better than a plow. It started with the pull of a cord, and the operator stood behind its metal body holding two handles, rather like a wheelbarrow. Satisfied that it would do the job, Dad bought one and loaded it onto the little trailer we hauled behind the car when going to Deerfield for the summer. Along with the round washing machine with its wooden wringer, and other items necessary for our eight-week stay, it bounced over the Molly Stark Trail road behind our black Pontiac.

I often tagged along when Dad was working, but I soon tired of watching him wrestle the rototiller. The monster was loud and clunky, and sometimes hard to guide, so I would go and find my sister to play a game for a while. It was more fun when it was time to plant. Then I could help drop seeds for corn, Swiss chard, carrots, squash, peas, green and pole beans, and spinach into the furrows and cover them with soil. I laughed when it was time to put the white paper "hot caps" over the tomato plants because they looked like little igloos.

One of my favorite things about the apple trees was how much fun they were to climb, with thick limbs reachable from the ground, and smaller ones going on up. Crotches made for places to sit and survey the scene over the orchard grasses, watching iridescent barn swallows swoop through the air, and bees working the tall pink hollyhocks near the big barn door. My best friend those summers was Bruce, the neighbor's grandson, who came to stay across the street. He was my age and we often climbed trees together, finally seeing who could jump off the highest branch to the ground. I don't think that my mother watched that particular activity, but Dad seemed okay, making an occasional joking remark such as, "I don't want to take you to the hospital today."

My mother would usually be in the big kitchen of the house, stoking a fire in the grand black four-burner wood stove. She was a good cook, serving the common New England fare of meat, potatoes (usually baked), and vegetables. Her forte was baking, and we always had dessert at both lunch and supper. The pies were the favorite, the crisscrossed crust of the cherry ones, and the high rounded ones full of blueberries that we had picked. By the first of August the canning operation was in full swing as well. Dad loved those days when the big blue enamel canning kettle jiggled on the stove, and we filled pint and quart jars with bright red tomatoes, cut green beans, corn cut from the cob, and pink applesauce.

I know that Dad was proud to have raised all this food, and to take home cardboard boxes full of it to carry us through the fall and winter months. The product that he talked the most about in later years was a jam. Mom had seen the recipe in a magazine. It combined coarsely chopped pieces of apples and pears in a sugary syrup that jelled to a light golden condiment for toast or homemade yeast rolls. From the first taste on a spoon, Dad loved that stuff. There were plenty of apples, and two kinds of pears. The Bosc tree produced tan rough-skinned pears; the little Seckel variety were smaller and more yellowish with smooth skin. Each year Dad would make sure that one of the boxes to be packed would be full of apple-pear jam.

When I think about that now, I see Dad's smile wrinkling the skin around his blue eyes and the corners of his mouth. I think that the jam he loved is a fitting symbol of sorts: the beautiful golden color and the sweetness parallel the attributes in his soul.

In Dad's later years, he and Agnes enjoyed canning lima beans and plums from Dad's garden.

For Old Times' Sake

WHEN I LEFT DAD to visit with Aunt Pearl in Brownville, she was a hundred and four years old. On her wall she had a fancy cane given to her by the state of Maine, recognizing her as its oldest citizen. Dad was a youngster at ninety-one, and together they had a wealth of stories and memories about the family over the years. Moreover they shared a desire to get out and do things. One of the things they decided to do during that October week was to take a picnic out to an old road that had been a popular spot years earlier.

They made some sandwiches, packed some pickles and a few cookies, and filled the old wicker basket with the hinged top. Napkins were folded into the tablecloth, coffee went into the thermos, they got some jackets and they were off in the rental car. After a couple of turns down country roads that dwindled into pastures, they found the road they had remembered. The tire tracks on that one lasted longer but soon there was grass growing between the ruts there too. (My grandmother would have insisted on turning right around at the first sight of that!) Driving as far as he dared, Dad stopped the car and they spread the picnic cloth in the tall grass.

When they were ready to leave, they gathered their things into the basket, and got into the sun-warmed car. Dad switched on the engine and began to back up, looking for a wide enough place to turn around. Finding a promising one, he shifted and pulled forward until a sudden crunching sound startled them both. They looked at each other apprehensively. Had Pearl been driving in those days (her family was immensely grateful that she was not) she would undoubtedly have uttered her characteristic words: "Oh, deah, what have I hit now?" I don't know what Dad said, but he got out to survey the scene. Bending to look underneath the car, he could see a rock which had been hidden by the grass but was now lodged under the car. He straightened up, took the driver's seat again and tried to back down off the rock. It took a couple of more tries to get free but they were soon headed back down the road to Milo. As they pulled into the service station, they were greeted by the friendly attendant.

"How can I help you today?"

"Well," Dad said, "we hit a rock on a back road, so we need to have you look at it."

"All right," said the young man with a smile, let's take a look."

Once the car was up on the lift, it was easy to see that oil was dripping from the damaged spot. "Oh, boy" said Dad.

"How far have you been driving this?" the man asked, noting the Massachusetts plates.

"Oh, just from the Brownville road," replied Dad, his blue eyes twinkling.

"Well, you're lucky you didn't dry 'er out completely," said the attendant, but he wasn't smiling.

As Dad related this to me later, I thought about how it might have been quite a disaster. I pictured the ninety-one-year-old with his hundred-four-year-old companion stuck in a forgotten field for who knew how long.

"Did anyone know where you were?"

"No," said Dad looking a bit sheepish. Pearl didn't wait long after they returned home to tell the story to friends and family, who scolded and tut-tutted and preached about safety and good sense. Dad just kept smiling. I'm sure he thought that no matter what the consequences might have been, he and Pearl would have taken them in stride. He was delighted to have had the adventure with her, and delighted in telling the story.

Dad with Aunt Pearl in Brownville, Maine

Taken by Dad's son-in-law Rick Foster in 2001,
this has always been a favorite portrait of my dad
—always my hero.

A Final Challenge

MY SISTER AND HER HUSBAND owned a timeshare condo near Jackson Hole, Wyoming for a number of years. They gathered there with their children and assorted friends many times, in all seasons. In the summer of 2000 they invited a cousin and his wife, Dad, and me to join them at Teton Village for a few days. Dad flew from the West Coast, where he was living at Valle Verde, a large retirement center in Santa Barbara, I rode with cousins Alan and Katherine from their home in Vancouver, Washington. The trip was a story in itself, as I sat in the extended cab seat of their truck with Amanda, the standard poodle, for the seventeen-hour journey.

In the spacious condo, Dad and I shared one of the downstairs bedrooms and the adjacent bathroom. It was there that I became aware that Dad was having some new health issues. He was in the bathroom often and for long periods of time. One evening, he said, "I have been having trouble going to the toilet for a while now." Not wanting to cross into too personal a territory, I was quiet for a minute. We didn't talk about bodily functions much in our family, so instead of asking for details, I asked how long he had been bothered. He replied "Oh, several months." When I asked if he had seen a doctor, he said he hadn't but was going to make an appointment when he got back to Santa Barbara. I began to imagine various things that could be wrong, including prostate cancer, and urged him to be seen as soon as possible. I didn't sleep very well for the rest of the trip.

It was clear that Dad tired easily, walking outside only short distances. He had trouble staying warm, probably because he had lost some weight. In spite of that, he maintained his genial presence, enjoying some delicious meals, including elk steak at one of the restaurants in town. He tried valiantly to spell words for games of Scrabble. My niece and nephew, Pam and Nathan, had fun calling him on the misspellings and words that he just made up. "Meese isn't a word? It should be! Then what is the plural of moose?" What a lot of fun!

I was still working full time then, so I returned home to a busy life, but stayed in touch with Dad, usually by telephone. He did go to the doctor and he underwent some tests. One of those resulted in a diagnosis of diabetes, a big surprise to all of us. But the more devastating news was that he also had colon cancer, and needed to have surgery as soon as possible. Arrangements were made for that to take place when Barbara could go to be with him, as she had a part-time job, and more free time than I.

Dad survived the surgery and spent a few days in the hospital, then returned to Valle Verde's health center to recuperate a bit more before returning to his apartment. He did not have as much energy as he would have liked, but he felt better, and was happy to resume caring for himself.

A couple of months after the surgery I went down to visit. Dad welcomed me with his big smile, open arms, and the familiar thump on the back. He reported managing pretty well and was a bit annoyed that a date had been set for a counseling session with the hospital social worker. We went together to meet her, a young woman who was full of energy and ready to be helpful.

"How are things going?" she asked cheerfully.

"Well," he said, "not as well as I expected."

"Oh, do you want to tell me what's wrong?"

"How long have you got?"

His response was so quick and so unexpected that I felt shock and sadness. "The surgery was supposed to restore normal bowel control. That hasn't happened. I now have to check my blood sugar and was supposed to get some help with diet. That hasn't happened. Almost everything you eat turns to sugar, so what am I supposed to do?"

I sat quietly listening to my father list complaints that I had never heard him voice before. I felt powerless, and reluctant to enter into the conversation. As we left the session together I thought that the only thing I might do would be to consult with the dietitian about acceptable foods.

Next morning at the table, blood test kit in hand, Dad looked up with a sigh and said, "This is not a good life." My heart lurched and I didn't know what to say. Like a good social worker, I managed, "I know it is hard. I'm sorry." At the same time I thought about some of the positive things that he would say if he were the listener. But it didn't feel right to me, trying to put a good face on his situation when what I was thinking was that he was right.

This was a lot harder than the times when Mom was not doing well, mostly because he was dealing with her situation, and I didn't have to. Dad had been the rock all my life. He was seldom ill and always drank life from a half-full glass. What should I be doing now? I wished that Barb were there with me. Dad completed the blood test, and I left the table to get dressed. Later in the week I flew back home and returned to work.

It was the following year, at the age of nearly ninety-one, when Dad said that he wanted to make one last fall trip to Maine. As we talked about it on the phone, he said he had been given a little more time and thought he could make the journey. I knew that he would need a companion and I had two incentives to go. I wanted to be with Dad and I wanted to see my dearest college friend who was fighting cancer. Since we lived across the country from each other, we could not visit often. After a lot of thought and with some trepidation, I decided to accompany Dad. It was the sixteenth of October, 2001 when we lifted off from the little Spanish-style airport in Santa Barbara and headed east to Logan Airport in Boston.

The flight went smoothly and we had a hot meal at the airport before renting a car and heading out of the city. Dad had traveled those roads enough times that he was familiar with the exits and entrances to turnpikes and freeways. I was glad to have him driving, which he did with no problem. In fact he seemed to be enjoying traveling north, beginning to see some of the fall reds and yellows in the leaves for which New England is famous.

At one point after we crossed into Maine, I got behind the wheel. Dad was navigating, and he directed me to turn left onto a country road near the small town of Newport. Assuming that we were headed to Milo, I drove several miles before he said, "I don't think this is right; we'd better stop." So I pulled the car over and headed back over the road we had driven. About half an hour later we stopped at a service station and learned where we needed to go. Dad was disgusted with himself for losing his way. I thought to myself that it was a sign of his age and forgetfulness, but I was happy to be on the proper last leg of our trip.

As we neared the town of Milo, things looked familiar to me as well, and we sailed on up the road to Brownville, where Aunt Pearl was waiting for us at her small apartment in a rural retirement community.

"Oh, I am so glad to see you both," she said, half-laughing as she hugged us and welcomed us inside. We shared tea and cookies at the small table, and I helped Dad set his things in the bedroom, opening out the hide-a-bed where he would sleep. We were tired so I said good night and went to a cousin's home for the night.

It was our plan to go separate ways for the remainder of the week. I flew to Portland to visit with my college roommate. After his visit in Maine, Dad was to fly to Boston and be met by my nephew Nathan who would accompany him to Denver. My sister Barbara would then travel with him from there back to Santa Barbara. Dad was extremely weak and tired, and it was a difficult trip, but he arrived back home where Barb immediately contacted hospice. She then called me and said I had better come so I could see him once more. That was a Sunday. By the time I arrived Monday, Dad was unable to eat or take medication, and was not fully aware of us. He slept most of Tuesday in the care of a hospice nurse and Barb's daughter, Pam. When evening came, and his breathing changed, I spoke to him, saying that if he were ready to "go on his journey," he could; Barb, Pam, and I were together and would be all right. I know he heard because a barely perceptible smile crossed his face before he let go. I know that he was also happy to have accomplished his final goal. I was glad that I had been there.

Ever the happy gardener

Requiem

O N THE EVENING after Dad's death, I walked up to the garden and sat by myself. I wanted time alone in the place he loved, and didn't have any other expectations. Within just a few minutes, however, the dove came, and I later wrote the following poem.

Mourning Dove

It came quietly over my head and landed on the wire
fence Dad had built for the lima beans, an ordinary
gray-brown dove.
Stepping sideways on the weather-beaten wood
frame,
It turned its head slowly to address me with its dark,
beady eye.

I am here with you. I see your pain. I will miss him
too, the man who cared for this hillside of ours.

He dug deep to foil the gophers and got corn and
beans, tomatoes and peas from this sorry excuse for
soil.
He lugged heavy loads of grass clippings up the
steep uneven path, bundled in blue plastic tarps
slung over his shoulders
Emptied them into his big, sturdy compost bins and
sighed.

He often smiled up here, paused to sit sometimes on the four by four that edged his garden bed.
Listened to us birds and reveled in this warm California sunshine. No one else will be that patient here; no more eighty-pound pumpkins will be trundled down the hill in a wheelbarrow to win a contest.

The rakes and shovels hanging against the wall will be taken elsewhere. They may be loved and well used, but their time here is over, same as mine will be, and yours. I'll miss him, though. I never was afraid of him. You could tell he was a gentle soul who shared this earth of ours with all comers. Didn't want to share it with the gophers, but he knew that their holes would be here now he's gone.

We can't stay here and mourn too long, you know. There are bugs to catch and things to pack.
You can hold and treasure things he had. I will just remember the sounds of his footsteps, water running from the hose, earth being turned over, and the beauty of his smiling spirit.

ACKNOWLEDGMENTS

I started this book about ten years ago, writing by hand in an unlined journal. During the years since I have learned a lot and been helped by countless people. Now it is time to thank them and invite them to rejoice with me as this project becomes a published book.

My sister Barbara Foster and her husband Rick were the first ones I talked with about Dad. They helped me think about his nature and the qualities which endeared him to so many people. In addition, I thank Barb for her help sorting through pictures and choosing from so much shared history.

Thanks to friend Margaret Walsh who invited me to join her writing group. The membership has changed over the years, and the support, input and wise criticism have been invaluable. My current colleagues, Jeanette, Jim, Louette and Tria continue to shape and improve my writing skills. Special thanks go to Jeanette Raleigh who designed and redesigned the cover to my satisfaction.

When I became really serious about publishing I was introduced to Judith Jones and Pilgrim Spirit Communications. Judy met with me over coffee and I quickly became convinced that I had found the right editor. She did not know what a technical klutz I am, but has worked with patience and grace to get us through all the steps. I appreciate her skill as an editor, value our association, and thank her greatly.

There are many other folks who have supported me with their interest and enthusiasm. To all who have heard me say repeatedly, "I'm writing a book about my Dad," thank you and here it is!